Adventures of Nutty and Twittle

OH nuts!

I LOST My Little Sister

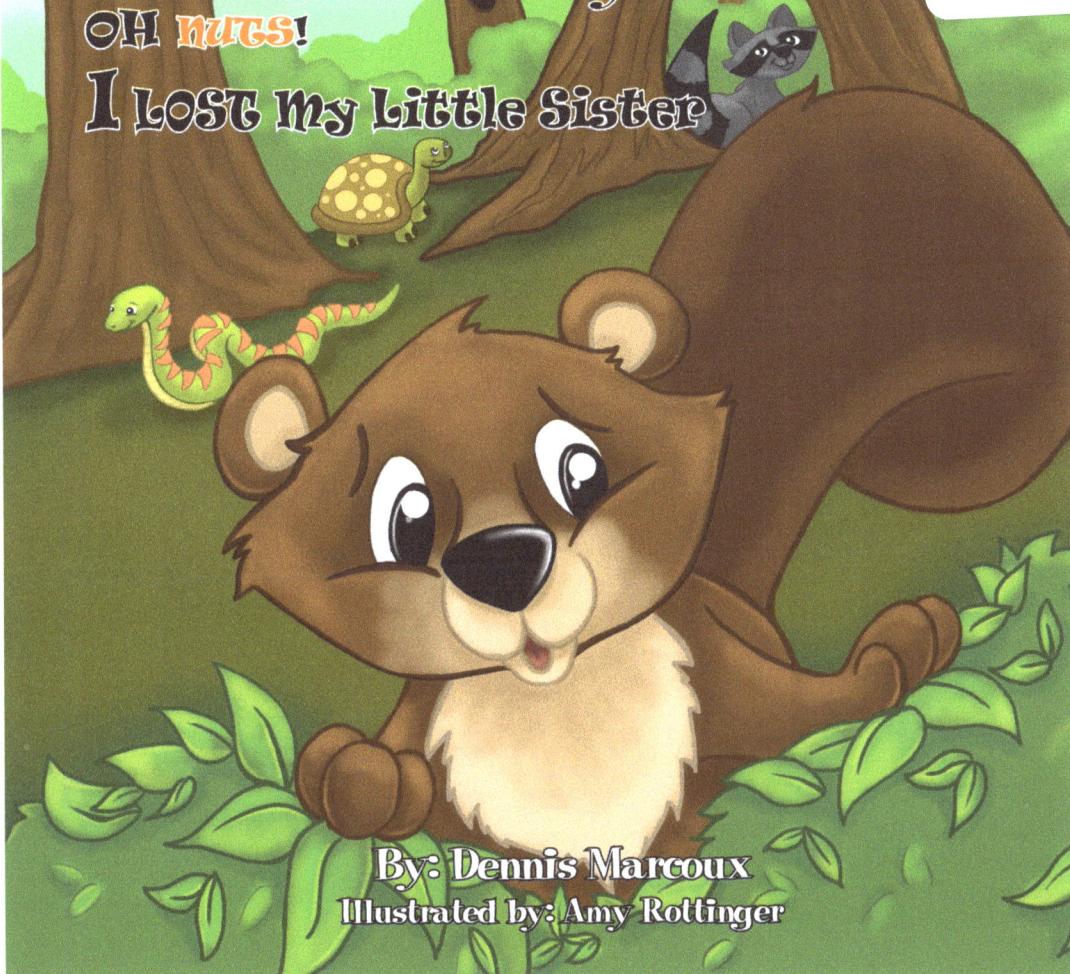

By: Dennis Marcoux

Illustrated by: Amy Rottinger

Halo
Publishing International

ISBN 13: 978-1-61244-274-7
Library of Congress Control Number: 2014917030

Printed in the United States of America

Halo
Publishing International
www.halopublishing.com

Published by Halo Publishing International
1100 NW Loop 410
Suite 700 - 176
San Antonio, Texas 78213
Toll Free 1-877-705-9647
www.halopublishing.com
www.holapublishing.com
e-mail: contact@halopublishing.com

For Molly who has been a joy and inspiration.
"I can fly; I can fly like a bird in the sky."
Love you forever to infinity.

And

In Memory of Ellie Rose, An angel who changed
my life and is always remembered.

WHY READ?

Dragons breathing fire, castles and kings,
this is the wonder that reading brings.
Words set your imagination free,
to sail like a pirate across the sea.
Soar in a spaceship across the sky
or chase a monster with one red eye.
Dance on a cloud, climb a snowy mountain
or search the desert for an ice cream fountain.
Meet cows that talk, trees that walk,
a giant climbing a magic beanstalk.
You'll find an adventure on every page,
it doesn't matter what your age.
Read every story, poem and rhyme.
Your mind will be growing all the time.

Nutty the squirrel and his friends fidgeted. It was the last day of school and they had great plans for the summer.

"Now don't forget. Be careful. Don't wander off by yourself. Remember the buddy system." Mrs. Hoot their teacher said. "And stay away from the Dark Forest. It's dangerous!"

The bell rang. "Hooray!" yelled Squinty the raccoon. Everyone ran outside.

Nutty the squirrel and his little sister Twittles lived closest to the school. They arrived home, ate their chocolate covered acorn snacks and got ready to play.

Speckles the turtle lived by the pond. It took him a long time to get home because he didn't move too fast. But today Speckles was going to Squinty's house for a sleepover. After stopping for snacks, Speckles and Squinty hurried to Nutty's house to play hide "n" seek with their friends.

Nutty and Twittles chittered and twitched their tails. Where were their friends?

Robby Robin was the first to arrive. He watched from high in the tree. "Here comes Wiggles. And Speckles and Squinty are right behind him."

Nutty gathered his friends together to explain the rules of the game. "First, Robby, you can't hide in the tree tops because no one else has wings and that wouldn't be fair."

Robby flicked his tail when he heard the rule, but he finally said, "Ok."

Rule number two was no peeking. They all agreed to that one.

"Ok, let's get started," said Nutty, his nose twitching with excitement. "I'll count to ten and you run and…"

"Hold on a minute," said Speckles, "I'm a turtle, remember? I don't move too swiftly. If you only count to ten, I will still be standing next to you when you open your eyes."

This time Nutty's tail flicked, but he knew Speckles was right. "Ok," he muttered, "I will count to twenty-five but no more than that."

Nutty was about to start the game when he noticed Twittles hanging back. "What's wrong Twittles?" asked Nutty.

"I don't think I want to play," she answered.

"Why?" Nutty asked.

"Because I always get found first, I never win," she answered.

Nutty looked at all his friends and thought what can I do?

Speckles broke the silence. "Twittles I have a feeling that today is going to be a lucky day for you."

"Really?" Twittles replied as her eyes opened wide.

"Really!" said Speckles.

Nutty covered his eyes with his paws and started counting. "One, two, three, four…." Everyone scrambled off to find their favorite hiding place. "Twenty-Five, ready or not here I come."

When Nutty uncovered his eyes and looked around, the first thing he noticed was a strange greenish rock covered with leaves. "I don't remember seeing that rock before." He crept towards it.

"Ouch!" yelped a voice.

Nutty jumped.

"You stepped on my head Nutty," said Wiggles.

"I'm sorry," Nutty said. "I didn't see you hiding in the grass, but I found you ha, ha!"

That's one Nutty thought as he moved toward the strange rock. He came right next to it and tapped on top. "Come out, come out whoever you are," he whispered.

"Aw gee," Speckles said. "How did you know it was me?" Nutty didn't pay much attention to what Speckles said. He wanted to find the rest of his friends. Two down and three to go, he thought.

Then something caught Nutty's eye. There was a bright orange spot in the blueberry bush. We don't have orange trees here, he thought. He dashed to the blueberry bush.

"Boo!" he shouted. There was a flutter and out popped Robby. "I saw your orange chest next to the blueberries. It was easy!" Nutty giggled.

"Only two left, Squinty and Twittles. Now where would a Raccoon hide? Ah ha, I think I know." Nutty ran across the yard to a hollow tree that had fallen during a winter storm. He leaped onto the tree and ran from one end to the other.

Finally he stopped and hanging upside down looked into the hollow tree. Two eyes with black all around them stared back.

"Gotcha!" he said. He laughed so hard he forgot he was upside down. "Oops!" he yelled as his paws slipped off the tree. Kerr Plunk! Nutty landed on his back in a pile of mushrooms.

Squinty popped out of the hollow tree. "Are you all right?" she asked.

"I'm fine. I knew it was you because of your black mask." Nutty rolled over and stood on his back legs. "Only Twittles left to find. This should be as easy as Turtle soup." Speckles' head snapped up. "I mean, I mean..." Nutty's voice cracked. "I mean mushroom pie."

Squinty, Speckles, Wiggles and Robby went back to Nutty's front porch. Nutty started looking for Twittles. He looked behind the trees, behind all the rocks, in the tall grass and bushes. No Twittles. He looked and looked. Where could she be? He began to worry. Did she go into the Dark Forest? Did she fall in the brook? Finally, he returned to his house without Twittles.

"Where is Twittles?" asked his friends.

"I don't know. I looked everywhere. Can you help me find her?"

Nutty remembered what Mrs. Hoot said earlier. "The Dark Forest can be a dangerous place, never wander off by yourself." Nutty was scared. "We have to find her. It's going to be dark soon."

"Stay calm," said Squinty. "We will help you."

"I will fly up to the sky," said Robby, "I can see the ground better from there. Speckles look inside the house. Wiggles look under the leaves, branches and grass. Squinty search behind the rocks and trees."

Nutty said, "I'll check the Dark Forest."

"Be careful, Nutty," said Speckles.

"I have to find her. It's my fault. I should never have let her go off by herself."

Speckles searched Nutty's house. He looked under the bed, in the closet and behind the doors. No Twittles.

Wiggles slithered through the grass over and over again. No Twittles.

Robby flew in circles, peering at the ground below. No Twittles.

Nutty approached the edge of the Dark Forest. "Twittles come out. We give up," he shouted. It was quiet. Nutty went deeper into the Dark Forest where the trees and brush grew closer together.

"What are you doing here?" growled a voice. Nutty stopped quickly. His head turned left then right trying to see where the deep voice came from.

He saw two bright yellow eyes staring at him. It was Plago the panther. "I'm here to find someone," said Nutty, trying not to show he was afraid.

"Who would that be?" asked Plago.

"Twittles, my little sister. We can't find her. We are afraid she is lost. Have you seen her?" Nutty said.

"No one has come into this part of the forest in a long time," Plago said. "And if you think I would harm her, you are wrong. Baby squirrels are too small for me to eat. However, big squirrels can be tasty."

Nutty, his heart pounding like a drum, turned and ran out of the Dark Forest all the way back to his house. Everyone was waiting to hear if Nutty had found Twittles. He told them what happened with Plago the panther. Nutty's friends sat in silence. Where could Twittles have gone? Where was she hiding?

Suddenly, Nutty heard a familiar sound.

"Hoot, Hoot!" Nutty and all his friends looked up at the sky. "Hoot, Hoot!" The voice came closer.

Above the trees they saw Mrs. Hoot, the wise old owl coming towards them. Everyone watched as Mrs. Hoot landed. She walked slowly keeping her eyes wide open, looking at each and every one of them. She moved right up to Nutty and said, "I believe I have something you lost." She lifted a wing and nestled under her feathers was Twittles.

Everyone jumped up with amazement. Then they smiled and hugged and squeezed Twittles so hard she could hardly breathe.

"Excuse me," Mrs. Hoot said with a firm voice. "Do any of you remember what I told you when you left the school house?"

Squinty, Speckles, Wiggles, Robby and Nutty hung their heads. They were afraid to look at their teacher. They knew they hadn't paid attention to what she told them.

"I found Twittles and you will never know where. You will always wonder where she was," Mrs. Hoot said, "and Twittles will never tell you. It will be her secret and mine."

Nutty lifted his head. "I'm sorry Mrs. Hoot. I guess we didn't listen. We just wanted to play. We promise it will never happen again."

The wise owl gazed at them one more time. Then she spread her wings, took a deep breath and flew off.

Nutty held Twittles' paws. "I am sorry Twittles. I won't let you out of my sight ever again."

"I know Nutty. I shouldn't have hid where I did." Then with a little smile on her face she said, "But I will never tell you my secret place. So don't ask!"

Do you know where Twittles was hiding?

www.ingramcontent.com/pod-product-compliance
Lightning Source LLC
LaVergne TN
LVHW070839080426
835511LV00025B/3481